MW01484866

11.11

ORACLE

ANSWERS TO UPLIFT AND SHIFT

ALANA FAIRCHILD

BLUE ANGEL® PUBLISHING

THE 11.11 ORACLE: ANSWERS TO UPLIFT AND SHIFT
Copyright © 2020 Alana Fairchild

Published by Blue Angel Publishing®
80 Glen Tower Drive, Glen Waverley
Victoria, Australia 3150
Email: info@blueangelonline.com
Website: www.blueangelonline.com

Edited by Jamie Morris & Leela J. Williams
Blue Angel is a registered trademark of Blue Angel Gallery Pty. Ltd.

ISBN: 978-1-925538-89-2

WHAT IS 11.11?

Recently, comedian Ellen DeGeneres said she had repeatedly seen 11.11 and decided it was a sign – that she had a flat battery! That made me laugh. But she's not far off the mark from my perspective.

Seeing 11.11 is about more than noticing a curious number pattern. It is a sign, but it is more than that, too. It is a vibration. It has a function, an action and a purpose. It is meant to awaken, uplift and inspire us, so we don't become overly earthbound. It teaches us how to be spiritually connected and open to possibilities. It is rebellious, loving, positive and wildly optimistic. 11.11 is the Universe saying over and over again, if something doesn't work, let's change it up for something vastly superior. 11.11 rarely indicates insignificant change. It initiates a complete overhaul in consciousness and experience. It may sound like that would take a long time to accomplish, but when you work with the 11.11

frequency a lot can happen in an instant because it is pure spiritual energy. And, spiritual energy operates beyond the confines of time and space.

The tired workings of ego drag us down emotionally, physically and psychologically. 11.11 is a cosmic recharge of our spiritual battery, giving us the inner boost we need to step up our spiritual game to a new level. Ego reinforces old patterns, lacks imagination and generally believes the worst about everything and everyone (including ourselves). 11.11 is the loving cosmic trickster playfully poking out its tongue at ego and saying, "How about this instead?"

Accessing the 11.11 frequency can be a relief and, at times, a challenge. By its very nature, it directly confronts the ego. Wherever we are trapped in lower frequencies— in fear, anger, shame, guilt and such—is where we will be stirred up as we begin to let go. Here, I will add that there is nothing wrong with lower-frequency experiences. Part of how we become empowered spiritual human beings is by undergoing the dark side of life. We can learn and grow from such experiences. It is only a problem when we get stuck in a negative loop and cannot break free.

That's when we need 11.11, and that's why it's so universal. Being human is not always easy. Our emotional patterns and psychological fabrications are both wonderful and terrible, constructive and destructive. We often tell each other the most awful stories about life, ourselves and other people. Listening and responding to the 11.11 frequency takes courage because what comes through is so out of harmony with mainstream consciousness.

The dominant thought patterns in our culture are fear-based and promote ideas of scarcity and separation. There is an overarching message that there is not enough for everyone, so we'd better get what we need and forget about others. The resulting competition pits us against each other and brings out the ugliest traits of human nature. In contrast, the 11.11 frequency can bring out the most beautiful qualities of the human spirit – freedom, trust, alignment with spiritual wisdom, healing, forgiveness, release, opening up to life as a healing adventure, and the capacity to attract what is needed in a way that benefits all beings, just to give you some examples.

When you tune into the 11.11 frequency and are learning to trust it, I can almost guarantee there will be moments when you wonder if you are completely crazy for doing so. That is usually an excellent sign that you are breaking free of mainstream conceptions and plugging into something more vital and alive – and much more real, too. As you free yourself from fear-based systems, the leap into a different way of being may make you feel you are courting insanity, but it is also beautiful and compelling. It provides relief, as the deeper part of your true self knows it is far more truthful than ego-driven horror stories mixed with delusions of grandeur.

Attraction to this frequency means a deeper empowerment

of your spirit is taking place. It is reaching out from your heart and reminding you there is another way, a better way to be human than the egos of this world have concocted. You are daring to be optimistic and hopeful and to believe in the power of inner healing and that positive energy holds great transformational potential.

You are willing to align yourself with something positive, bright, supportive, encouraging, loving and fearless. You have the courage, the curiosity and the wisdom to do this.

Allow your soul to soak up these 11.11 frequencies as if they are the scent of a sacred tea and picking up this oracle is like settling down for a divine tea party with Spirit. Give yourself permission to recognise the pain of the ego-created beliefs and experiences you have been holding on to without judgement. It is all part of the human journey. Also, as you have found your way to this book, at least part of you wants to heal, be inspired, live without being held back by fear and trust that the Universe is loving, wise, generous and wants to look out for you and offer you the time of your life!

When you read one of the messages in answer to a question you have, notice your inner response before your logical mind kicks in and tells you all the (mainstream-consciousness generated) reasons it is nonsense. If you are of a particularly sceptical bent, that's fine. When I've worked with sceptical people in the past, I've always offered this suggestion: "Why not treat it as an experiment, and see what happens in your life when you accept the idea?" The reports I have received from the spiritual 'scientists' willing to give this whole '11.11 thing' a go, have been most heart-warming.

Every instance of 11.11 is the Universe reassuring us. Every 11.11 encounter is the Universe encouraging us to believe in the goodness that is possible and available – should we be loving, wild and wise enough to allow it to rule our hearts and minds. And every 11.11 is a reminder from the cosmic trickster that if we think it's all going to hell in a handbasket, it's time to invite the Universe to show us a more loving and inspired reality. It is also broadcasting that everything is going to be okay.

You can say the following invocation to tune into the 11.11 frequency whenever you wish. Before consulting this book, when your ego is making you miserable or when you want to reinforce the knowledge that the good and true will overcome all negativity in your heart and the world, say:

I am open to the unconditionally loving grace primed to support me in my most beautiful, uplifting, inspired life. With mercy and compassion, please clear my path so I may be empowered to grow with trust, courage and joy. Thank you for the blessings that flow to all beings with such abundance. May there be grace, protection and divine assistance so all may receive their highest good. So be it.

HOW TO PLAY
WITH THE 11.11 ORACLE

The 11.11 Synchronicity Session

Here are five simple steps to freedom for when you have a question and want the oracle to answer you with a number transmission.

1. Centre yourself in your heart.

2. Ask your question.

3. Close your eyes and randomly flip open a page, letting the index finger of your non-dominant hand land upon a page.

4. Read your answer (the closest number to where your finger landed).

5. Reflect, heal, shift, awaken.

The Number Interpretation Session

When you want to clarify the meaning of a number you keep seeing, follow these simple steps.

1. Centre yourself in your heart.

2. Clear your mind of what you think your number means.

3. Look up the number you keep seeing. If you need further insight, you can also look up variations of the number. If you see 1088, you can also read the insight for 10, 88, 108, 1, 0, and 8. Just be careful not to overwhelm yourself with too much information – the message from one number will often be enough.

4. Read your answer.

5. Reflect, heal, shift, awaken.

THE MESSAGES

I choose to take steps that align me with my higher self.

I connect to my higher self and experience an inflow of help, guidance and support.

I create and attract positive energy.

I make practical choices that honour my inspired intentions.

5 I trust in the goodness of change.

I trust in the love the Universe has for me.

7 I trust myself.

I take complete responsibility for myself, and in doing so, find the freedom to live as I choose.

9

I choose
to let go.

10 The Universe blesses a new venture, project or chapter in my life.

11 I upgrade my beliefs, attitudes and expectations to a higher frequency, thus evoking a positive shift in myself and the reality I am co-creating.

12 I open my heart to new connections, partnerships and ways of relating that honour individuality and mutuality.

13 I reach out playfully, creatively and authentically to engage with new communities.

I ground my plans and visions into reality with conscious action.

My inspired actions set change in motion and lead me toward breakthrough and freedom. 15

 My actions are wisest when they are in harmony with my heart.

I honour my intuition by acting on its guidance. 17

18 I claim my empowerment by recognising I am responsible for and free to make my own decisions.

I align my actions to Spirit and surrender my attachment to outcome. **19**

20 I accept divine blessing, healing and protection for all relationships, according to a higher loving purpose.

I balance intimacy, connection and independence. **21**

22 I co-create through sacred partnerships based on mutual enhancement, affinity and trust.

23 Together, we generate the energy and inspiration to create positive resources which benefit the collective.

24 The Universe supports me as I manifest the divine beauty of my true life path.

25 My relationships generate powerful change and provide opportunities for inner healing and soul growth.

26 I open my heart to loving relationship.

I attract healing energy into my relationships. **27**

28 My relationships empower me.

I find stimulation and support for my
spiritual journey in my relationships. **29**

30 My creative expression honours my soul
and adds value to the collective.

31 When others look to me for leadership,
I tap into an inner well of creativity,
practicality and inspiration.

32 I relate to others from a creative,
spontaneous inner place that encourages
freedom for all.

33 I choose to devote myself to my heart's
highest purpose.

As I express my creativity, there is an increase of clarity, healing and practical blessings in my life.

I attract new avenues for healing change and manifestation through creative expression.

 My heart opens and attracts the blessings of the Universe.

I naturally generate healing energy.

38 My creative expression reaches many people and brings light into this world.

39 My creativity and self-expression support the release of old energies with grace and healing.

40 There is always a loving, divine order at work for the greater good.

41 I embrace the new phase that is now awakening in my life.

I commit to my relationships with trust in the divine plan unfolding between us.

 I commit to my creative self-expression, and in doing so, awaken a helpful healing process within my soul.

 I open my heart to the powerful divine support from loving angels that helps me in all aspects of my spiritual and physical life.

 Loving angelic assistance encourages me to create more freedom through change, growth and new direction.

46 Angelic energy gently inspires my heart to open and receive greater love and material abundance in my life.

47 I open my heart to the powerful spiritual support of loving angels who help me trust my intuition and tune into my innate healing abilities with confidence.

48 My open heart attracts angelic assistance that helps me step into my power and realise my inner spiritual authority.

49 Angelic energy heals my heart, now, so I can consciously perceive my higher guidance.

50 I surrender my resistance to change with complete trust in the loving workings of a higher plan.

51 In allowing change, I accept new blessings to my life.

52 I embrace healthier patterns and increased personal responsibility in my relationships.

53 It is safe for me to be seen as the unique person I am.

54 Change flows into my life as the practical manifestation of divine blessing.

55 Divine disruptions and pattern breakers lovingly support a more beautiful reality for all concerned.

56 I trust in love's unpredictable healing journey.

57 I trust my unexpected and surprising insights.

I am ready, willing and courageously claiming my rightful place in the world.

Radical change brings the possibility of a new and blessed reality.

 I am capable of unconditional love.

I am worthy of unconditional love.

I choose to bring unconditional love to my relationships.

 I joyfully enhance, create and express love in my communities.

 By trusting my heart, my most beautiful life path manifests.

 Healing change is awakening in my heart, ushering a new emotional reality into being.

I accept the generous blessings of love and abundance in my life with gratitude, joyful that I have more to share with others.

My heart knows the way to go.

 I trust in the powerful wisdom of my heart.

I allow my heart to release all attachment to the past and be open to renewal and spiritual rebirth.

70

I trust the
Universe.

71 At all times, my inner knowing inspires me to take the most favourable course of action.

72 I bring positive healing energy into my relationships.

73 I trust my intuition to guide my connections with others.

74 My body and my life are now healing.

75 My inner wisdom brings healing change to my life.

76 I walk the way of wisdom, choosing to live to my soul values and the knowledge of my heart.

77 I forgo judgement and seek higher understanding and the truth that sets me free.

78 My intuition lovingly guides me to the most constructive ways of asserting my true self.

79 As I heal, trust and allow Spirit to guide me, I discover a way of grace.

80 The Universal Mother has a loving plan for me to manifest my soul and attain spiritual fulfilment.

81 I empower myself by taking responsibility for my experiences and trusting that everything unfolds in my life for a positive purpose.

82 I choose to empower myself in my relationships.

I take responsibility for my creativity and wellbeing.

I am responsible for my empowered attitude to my body and physical wellbeing and trust that I can heal.

I respond to change in a way that benefits myself and others.

I respect love's wisdom and power.

87 My intuition is a powerful and constructive guide.

As I align myself with higher will, I open my heart and mind to the successful manifestation of my soul purpose. **88**

89 I defer all matters to Spirit's higher will and become wise in my expression of leadership.

Spirit is enacting a higher plan for the greatest good, and I choose to trust it unconditionally.

91 An ending in my life is a sign of karmic completion and release from which a bright new era shall begin.

92 Spirit now offers healing and grace for twin-flame connections and soulmate relationships.

93 It is part of my spiritual journey to express myself creatively.

94 I offer all issues and concerns to the protective and healing grace of Spirit.

95 I trust the flow of spiritual goodness in my life, especially when life is heading in unexpected directions.

I let go of my attachments and allow love to flow freely. **96**

97 I am open to my inner healing channel through which spiritual grace flows generously for the greatest good of all.

I offer my desires and plans in service to a higher loving truth that works through me for the greater good.

With gratitude, I embrace karmic healing, karmic release and the ending of a cycle so I can arise anew according to divine timing and purpose.

My spirit is ignited by the Universe and open to a powerful fresh start.

 I embrace the spirit of the divine child within my heart and allow myself to be playful, curious and open to life.

I choose to strengthen my uniqueness by sharing my authentic self with others.

103 There is a higher loving intelligence flowing through me, inspiring creativity and the playful freedom to be myself and shine my light.

104 I align myself with the divine plan for my life, taking practical steps with patience and commitment and allowing the way to unfold.

105 I choose to trust the divine design unconditionally. Its clarity will reveal itself in due course.

106 As I open my heart, I am aware of emotional pain and allow it to heal and release. My heart becomes more spacious and emotionally ready to receive new blessings of grace.

107 I open and trust my spiritual channel to receive the healing wisdom of the Universe.

108 I am a divine being, in the protection of spiritual grace and empowered to create positive influence for the greater good.

109 When I sincerely ask the Universe to heal an issue in my life, I am guided to take steps that bring about resolution, release and happiness.

110 A new and divine chapter is awakening in my life, one that has been predestined to facilitate my higher purpose.

Through inspired intention, I align myself with the infinite generosity, genius and grace of the Universe.

Inspired new patterns of connection encourage positive shifts in my relationships.

I am a creative powerhouse of inspiration who brings fresh energy to our collective.

With patience and courage, I allow the practicalities and structures of my life to shift according to a higher plan.

115 I refocus my mindset toward the higher frequencies of freedom, love and liberation.

116 I gratefully receive blessings of divine alignment in matters of the heart for healing any issues to do with finance and abundance.

117 I am inspired to trust and align myself with the wisdom, love and limitless healing of the Universe.

118 I am empowered to manifest a path of personal and spiritual growth.

119 I am inspired to surrender, let go and allow for endings that bring about new beginnings.

120 I align my intentions with the greatest good and take inspired initiative in my relationships.

121 A balance of solitude and intimacy brings a fresh beginning to my relationships.

122 I am supported by the higher plan and loving healing purpose that unfolds through all my relationships.

123 A phase of accelerated evolution lifts me to the next level of my spiritual manifestation.

124 I attract sacred connections that foster the health of my body, mind and soul.

125 Remaining in my truth while connecting with others, brings healing change.

126 Speaking my truth allows for deep healing heart connections.

127 Being my true self evokes healing for all.

I grow by assuming personal responsibility
in my relationships. **128**

129 I gracefully release any relationships that have
run their course with forgiveness in my heart.

My intentions begin the loving creation of
a new reality. **130**

131 My desired reality evolves as I work on myself.

132 I playfully contribute loving consciousness to my relationships.

133 I ask for divine guidance and receive answers to my prayers.

134 I ask for divine guidance and recognise physical signs that my prayers are answered.

135 Healing change begins with me.

136 I attract love by being loving, especially toward myself.

137 I am on a powerful and creative healing journey.

138 I choose to revitalise my spirit and inspire my heart by making time for play.

139 I use simple, loving rituals and creative self-expression to acknowledge and release the past.

140 I connect with the angels and shelter in their loving and powerful protection and guidance.

141 From intention to action, I set my life path in motion.

142 I attract supportive connections and partnerships that are mutually beneficial.

143 As I walk my path, opportunities are created, and connections open to me.

With each step I take, my divine path becomes clearer. **144**

145 I trust in the shifting direction of my life path as I am shielded and protected by the angels.

I have the courage to live from my heart. **146**

147

My life is a healing journey
that I take with trust.

148 I am gaining spiritual mastery and respectfully acknowledge my progress.

149 I bravely let go of what no longer serves my path.

150 I embrace the loving, wild and unpredictable nature of my spiritual journey with unconditional trust.

151 I accept a rapid succession of positive changes in my life.

152 Changes in my relationships bring about a new chapter in my life.

153 My influence in communities evokes healing change.

154 My presence evokes true spiritual freedom for all.

155 My clear intention to evolve attracts divine guidance, support, protection and intervention for my highest good.

156 My clear intention to become freer stimulates an awakening of the heart.

157 My positive intentions bring about healing change.

158 My authenticity destabilises false systems and unveils the path to loving empowerment.

159 As I surrender and align myself with love, I become a vehicle for spiritual healing in this world.

160 My heart is capable of a new and deeper experience of love.

161 I open my heart to fresh beginnings in love.

162 My open heart increases the presence of love in my relationships.

163 In remaining open to life, I attract and create great abundance.

164 In following my heart, I attract material and spiritual blessings for the benefit of all.

165 When I give up the desire to control, I allow love to flourish, and I become free.

166 My clear intention to be aligned with love attracts material and spiritual blessings for the greatest good of all.

167 My compassion brings healing to this world.

168 I send love and healing prayers to those in positions of authority and power.

I trust in the heart's wisdom and ability to heal through spiritual grace. **169**

170 I initiate thoughts and prayers of healing for the greatest good of all.

I accept my role as a healing channel and light bearer on this planet. **171**

172 I effectively support others on their healing journey, facilitating a deeper connection to their inner truths.

I encourage my tribes and communities to embrace healing. **173**

174 I pray for healing for all beings so they may manifest their true spiritual destiny.

Living with trust and confidence in Spirit inspires others to trust in the healing potential of change. **175**

176 My confidence in the wisdom of the heart inspires others to seek and trust their own hearts' wisdom.

177 As I set my intention to be a healing presence in this world, I align with the great healing power of the Universe.

178 Earth Mother generously provides me with all I want and need for my healing journey.

179 Spirit provides me with all I need for my spiritual growth so that I may manifest divine beauty in the world.

180 Through divine blessing and a twist of fate, I step into an era of profound empowerment.

My inner power is evolving into a higher level of expression. **181**

182 I take initiative and responsibility in my relationships and am a source of inspiration for healthy and mature connections.

I step joyfully into my role as a wise guide within my soul tribe. **183**

184 I demonstrate spiritual authority in my life by taking responsibility for my actions.

I assume complete responsibility for my personal freedom. **185**

186 I assume spiritual responsibility for the love I generate and experience.

I self-validate my intuition and inner knowing. **187**

188 My clear intentions evoke divine blessing in the spiritual and material worlds for my complete fulfilment and the benefit of all beings.

I attract divine intervention and protection through active spiritual practice. **189**

190 I take steps to tie up loose ends and peacefully allow a cycle to end to create space for the new.

I seed new beginnings as I resolve and release the past. **191**

192 As I let go, I am empowered to create something fresh and new.

193 My intention for divine healing and protection for all attracts an inflow of generous spiritual grace to my community.

194 I initiate spiritual intervention for the greater good of all.

195 I ask Spirit to bring healing change in accord with the highest wisdom and greatest good of all.

196 Through my spiritual connection to the Universe, unconditional love pours forth to bring comfort to all beings.

I tune into the healing frequencies of the Universe and bring light to all in need. **197**

198 Through my spiritual connection to the Universal Mother, I invoke blessings of abundance for myself and all beings in need of her generosity and protection.

I ask for karmic healing and complete resolution through forgiveness and spiritual grace in all matters that no longer serve my soul growth. **199**

200 The Universe is my co-creating partner, manifesting miracles and generating grace for all beings, including myself.

201 I trust the Universe as my loving partner as I embrace the beginning of a fresh chapter.

202 I heal and grow through the sacred contracts of my relationships.

203 As I honour my connection to the Universe, I create an inflow of resources and inspired energies into my communities.

204 My inner spirituality supports my relationships, and my relationships support my divine life path.

As I progress in my spiritual journey, my relationships evolve to new levels of freedom. **205**

206 My relationships provide blessed opportunities to learn and express unconditional love.

I allow myself to heal and grow through conscious connection with others. **207**

Through conscious relationships, I allow myself
to practice being lovingly in my power.

My connection with my spiritual guides is
powerful, helpful and real.

 Soulmate connections awaken and stimulate
my authentic self.

Soulmate connections support me in being more
of myself and accelerate my spiritual growth.

212 As I give and receive equally, my relationships mature and evolve.

213 I allow my relationships to positively mirror my authentic self, boost my self-esteem and help me recognise my worth so that I can express my creativity with ease and confidence.

214 My relationships inspire me to persevere toward my true life path.

215 I allow change to flow into my life through my relationships, bringing benefit to all.

216 Life provides me with the relationships I need for beautiful heart awakenings.

217 The Universe serves my highest and greatest good by providing me with relationships that are catalysts for inner healing.

218 I attract the right connections, at the right time, to manifest my destiny for the mutual benefit of all.

219 As I take my relationship journey, I trust in the greater guiding wisdom that brings healing and evolution for the benefit of all.

220 I trust in the divine plan as I co-create my dreams with the loving support of the Universe.

I trust in divine timing. **221**

222 I am open to the higher healing purpose of my relationships, including soulmates, twin flames and other soul connections, and welcome an inflow of healing grace.

As I honour my life path, I inspire my soul tribe to live with boldness, creativity and trust. **223**

224 I trust the Universe to make adjustments in all areas of my life, so I am aligned with my true path and divine destiny.

225 I embrace the unexpected as a sign the Universe is blessing and aligning me with my true life path.

226 My heart is a magnet for the blessings of divine prosperity, love and abundance that further my life path.

227 I seek the higher perspective of divine truth, which frees me from judgement and connects me to practical healing wisdom.

I confidently approach the challenges that arise, knowing I am only given what I have the capacity to handle and transform into wisdom.

I gratefully accept the awakening of past-life talents and abilities that support my current life journey.

 Through sacred connections and my soul tribe, a new era is being born.

Through a sacred connection to my soul tribe, I discover my deeper and more authentic self.

232

I choose playful, creative, respectful relationships that are mutually beneficial and mutually enhancing.

I intuit authentic, helpful spiritual guidance
as I tune into my heart.

The Universe provides me with loving
connections to help manifest my life path
for the greatest good of all.

 I honour changes in my sacred partnerships
and soul tribes as a healthy sign of growth.

I connect with my heart and increase the
presence of love in my sacred partnerships
and soul communities.

237 I belong, I matter, and I am worthy of divine support, protection and respectful connections.

238 I choose conscious mirroring in my connections with others, where differences and respective paths are honoured.

239 Spirit provides unconditional blessings and karmic healing for all relationships to fulfil their divine destiny and higher healing purpose.

240 Through my relationships, I find stability and grounding that supports me in manifesting my destiny.

241 Through my conscious connections with others, I choose to explore and express a healthy balance of independence and togetherness.

I grow the substance and stability of my relationships through intimacy. **242**

243 Creative solutions emerge when I express my authentic self.

The angels are sending help to heal and evolve all relationship matters.

245 My enduring connection with Spirit allows me to accept change with serenity in my heart.

246 I experience rapid progress in areas of connection, physical wellbeing, abundance and love.

247 I attract the best people, information and opportunities to create healing on all levels of my being and all areas of my life.

248 Mother Earth generously supports me so that I may manifest my spiritual destiny.

249 Gracefully embracing the ending of a relationship or pattern of relating leads to freedom, increased energy and inner peace.

I allow space for divine energy to flow into my relationships, creating deep and healing change. **250**

251 Changing my approach to my relationships evokes a positive chapter in my life.

Mutual and authentic sharing invites breakthrough. **252**

253 Honest self-disclosure creates new avenues for expression, healing and connection.

254 I embrace unpredictable changes, as I recognise they bring healing and establish a more secure and stable foundation for my life.

255 Surrendering my relationships to the highest divine energies brings spiritual progress and healing transformation for all.

256 I am willing to change and heal the way I view and express love.

257 I am willing to heal the way I view and express partnership.

I take full responsibility for the quality of my relationships and become free of past patterns.

259 I invite the Universe to mercifully manifest karmic healing in my connections, with love.

I choose to open my heart and respect what I feel.

261 I create new beginnings in my relationships through heart-centred intimacy.

I allow myself to be loved. **262**

263 I allow myself to belong.

I allow myself to be present. **264**

265 Whilst in devotion to others, I give myself permission to be fully myself.

In sacred partnership, a positive shift in material abundance and emotional wellbeing flows for the benefit of all. **266**

267 Healing energies enter my relationships, redefining and revitalising what it is to love and be loved.

Gratitude for all I have, amplifies the blessings flowing into my life, now. **268**

269 I am capable of attracting and experiencing deeply spiritual connections with others.

I attract the perfect teachings, teachers, information and guides at the perfect time and in the perfect way. **270**

271 I discern my truth with gratitude and respect for all the teachings given to me.

I have valuable insights to share and remain open and committed to continual learning. **272**

273 I joyfully contribute my inner resources to my communities.

I make commitments that feel truthful and resonate for me. **274**

275 I relax in the face of upheaval and change in my relationships, understanding that this is a natural part of the evolution process.

My spiritual journey increases the activity and healing power of love in my relationships and the world. **276**

277 As I heal myself, I bring healing energy
into my relationships.

278 I sustain my spiritual journey by practising
conscious connections with myself and others.

279 I am open to past-life healing, in all my
relationships, as needed for the greater good.

280 I allow divinely ordained and powerful
connections to have a positive impact on my life.

281 I prioritise and assume responsibility in my relationships in a way that respects myself and others.

282 I effortlessly attract empowering connections.

283 I effortlessly attract and recognise my soul tribe according to divine grace and timing.

284 With gratitude, I acknowledge my material blessings which continue to grow through empowering connections.

285 As I open to empowering relationships, my world rapidly and positively changes.

286 I know how to express power with wisdom and love.

287 I attend to those within my care with wisdom.

288 I gratefully accept the abundant and empowering relationships that contribute to my success for the greatest good of all.

289 Sometimes I need to say no so I can say yes to a more beneficial and constructive long-term outcome.

290 I pray that karmic healing in my relationships brings clarity and freedom, through mercy and kindness for all.

291 In letting go of what I think I know, I open myself to spiritual intervention that brings new understanding and constructive wisdom.

292 With gratitude, I allow my relationships to evolve through shifting stages of commitment.

293 I recognise the impact my relationships have in the world and ask for spiritual blessing, healing and protection for all.

294 I ask for blessing, healing and protection as shifts in my relationships evoke transformation in myself and my life.

295 I invoke blessing, healing and protection so that karmic resolution can create freedom in my relationships.

296 I invoke blessing, healing and protection so that forgiveness can create peace in my relationships.

297 I invoke blessing, healing and protection so that deeper understanding of my relationships can create wisdom.

I invoke blessing, healing and protection to bring mutual empowerment and emotional fulfilment to my relationships. **298**

299 I surrender my attachment in my relationships into the loving embrace of Universal healing so the highest resolution may be found, to benefit all.

I allow the Universe to work through my body, mind and soul so I may be a creative instrument of divine grace, healing and light in this world. **300**

I deepen my inner spiritual awakening through creative self-expression, which in turn stimulates a fresh start and clear direction in my life.

I patiently gather and synthesise information from numerous sources, distilling and unifying wisdom and attracting a new path.

I open myself to the divine inspiration and joyful creativity that increase healing and happiness in my life and this world.

I anchor and ground the presence of my higher self into my heart, inviting spiritual wisdom, light and love to transform myself and my world.

305 My spontaneous approach to life rapidly transforms obstacles into stepping stones on my spiritual path.

I accept and am nurtured by my spiritual bond with communities that honour love's wisdom. **306**

307 I belong to a spiritual tribe of healers and guides who operate for the evolution and healing of humanity.

I inspire and lead by example. **308**

309

I hold space for endings to heal so new patterns can emerge within my communities.

310 I say YES to divine inspiration!

311 I rapidly transcend old ways, previous identities and outmoded belief systems and rest into a more loving, high-frequency way of being.

312 I boldly reach out for connection.

313 I choose to be happy in the present moment and, in doing so, create happier pathways for my future unfoldment.

314 My spirit guides and masters lovingly support and protect me on all levels.

315 My steps toward positive change lead me closer to freedom.

316 My inner optimist, playful heart and sense of humour create positive energy that attracts innovation and opportunities to my world.

317 I trust in the power of my inner spiritual gifts.

318 I can generate material abundance and live according to my definitions of success.

319 My choice to connect with others invites new energies to my life, brings about the end of a cycle and inspires a new chapter.

320 I activate divine purpose in my relationships by choosing a playful, generous approach.

I ground my creative visions in this world and bring them to life through my own initiative. **321**

The Universe provides me with all I want and need to bring my heart's desire to fruition, at the perfect time and in the perfect way.

I choose to interact with others in a way that increases energy levels for all.

 I express my authentic feelings through clear and grounded interactions.

I join forces with like-minded people, and with the power of group energy, we heal old patterns.

326 I give myself permission to receive genuine love, respect and admiration.

I work through the challenges in my relationships, and in doing so, unleash an abundance of creative, positive, healing energy. **327**

328 I choose conscious connections that foster mutual empowerment.

I invite spiritual energy into my connections with others, allowing for the miraculous and beautiful to happen. **329**

An important divine message is on its way to me, and I remain open to sensing it in my heart.

The Universe encourages me to say YES to new ideas.

 The Universe inspires me to say YES to soul-aligned partnerships.

You are connecting with a loving group of high-level spiritual guides who will help you fulfil your life path, as you confidently tune into your heart and feel for their wisdom.

The Universe loves that I take practical steps toward manifesting my heart visions in the world.

 The Universe invites me to do something different, to break free from routine and allow fresh energy to flow into my body, mind and life.

 The Universe is letting me know that love always finds a way.

 A challenge in my life is a sign my soul is healing, and I continue to trust in my journey.

I have the inner power and spiritual resources to sustain myself and move through any difficulties with grace.

A significant cycle is coming to an end, and a new day shall dawn.

 I implement strategy, practical steps and flexible plans to ground my creative ideas in the world.

Creative expression helps me discover my life purpose and true, authentic self.

342 Taking steps to express myself creatively helps me share my authentic self with others for true, rewarding intimacy.

A creative, playful approach generates inspired solutions and attracts new opportunities.

343

344 My friendship with the angels flows from my trusting heart and opens the way for support, protection and blessings.

I break free from controlling energies, within and around me, through creativity and playfulness.

345

346 As I freely and playfully express my creative self, I become aware of the deeper wisdom, truth and helpful guidance of my heart.

I heal myself and others through creative and authentic expression. **347**

348 I choose to validate my creative journey.

I ground beautiful spiritual energies through my creative offerings. **349**

I expand my inner and outer horizons
through creative expression.

I acknowledge what I have learned, distilling what
resonates most for my soul and stepping forth on my
path with the courage of my convictions.

 My inner connection with the Universe helps
me break free from social conditioning and mass
consciousness that does not resonate with my soul.

I am a dream-maker and co-creator of
loving cultural stories that heal and move
humanity forward.

After even my most challenging experiences, I acknowledge that I am here, I am breathing and the extraordinary inner power of forgiveness will set me free.

My spontaneous, authentic and creative self-expression is a catalyst for healing change in myself and the world.

My spontaneous, authentic and creative self-expression is a catalyst for heart healing within myself and in the world.

My spontaneous, authentic and creative self-expression is a catalyst for clarity, insight and wisdom for myself and others.

My spontaneous, authentic and creative self-expression helps me set firm, loving boundaries that respect the soul.

My authentic self-expression liberates me from an outmoded era, increasing my abundance and prosperity.

359

As I tune into my heart, my true creativity awakens and allows me to choose how I wish to live and what beliefs I shall cultivate.

As I listen to my heart, a new pathway miraculously opens before me, leading me to where I am destined to be, according to divine timing.

361

The Universe encourages me to acknowledge my deepest heartfelt passions so their power can attract what I want and need for spiritual fulfilment.

The power of my heart's true devotion shifts my consciousness and my reality, creating a way where a path was previously unknown.

 My heart light makes a positive difference in the world.

My light holds a frequency of love so others can feel supported on their spiritual journey.

366 I have confidence in my ability to create and attract material abundance and spiritual light.

367 I shine my heart light freely and unconditionally, offering spiritual comfort for all in need and attracting spiritual protection and support for myself, too.

368 My heartfelt life choices are a true way to attain fulfilment for the greatest good.

369 As I live in harmony with my inner spiritual journey, I effortlessly experience expansion, blessings, grace and protection.

370 Patiently allowing time and space for the integration of my experiences empowers my destiny and keeps me on my divine path.

371 Giving myself time and space to process my experiences leads to clarity and rapid progress.

372 I seek generous support in processing and integrating my experiences, which leads to rapid progress on my path.

373 I am patient with my healing process, giving myself time and space to fully integrate my experience, which in turn allows me to truly grow and transform.

374 As I digest my experiences with time and patience, I heal from within, creating transformation in my outer world.

I give myself the complete freedom to take my healing journey with unconditional trust and patience for the process. **375**

376 I commit to the wellbeing and freedom of my heart.

As I focus on my personal healing journey, my capacity as a healer and light bearer for others increases dramatically. **377**

378 As I walk my talk, I gain spiritual empowerment through my authentic experiences.

379 As I approach the end of a cycle, I give myself space to integrate the lessons and heal into readiness for a brighter chapter of my life.

380 By respecting my need for authenticity, truth and connection to myself and others, I am empowered to fulfil my destiny.

381 I invoke the divine feminine to heal and bless my life through her grace, creativity, beauty and power.

382 Honouring my soul truths creates an abundant flow of spiritual blessings in my life.

I take responsibility for creating joy in my life.
383

384 I cultivate playfulness to discharge negative energy, to ground my spirit in my body and to open me to infinite blessings.

I welcome the many good things that flow into my life when I trust the unexpected.
385

386

My heart knows how to attract good things, so I care for, listen to and nurture my heart.

I trust the unique inner perfection of my
soul journey.

 I attract good fortune, supreme spiritual
protection and divine blessings, which I
effortlessly share for the greatest good of all.

 I choose to step into a new level of personal
empowerment and spiritual responsibility and attract
an increased flow of spiritual grace to my life.

I choose to believe in grace.

By transcending the past, I transform
myself and my life.

I am capable of creating and attracting
relationships that operate on a refined
frequency of unconditional love and respect.

What I want, the Universe wants for me,
and we manifest healing magic and divine
beauty, together.

Divine grace ensures that my visions
transform into reality.

395 Divine intervention brings breakthroughs, so my creative inspirations are fulfilled for the greater good.

396 Group endeavours based on heart wisdom attract powerful spiritual energy and protection for their true purpose.

397 I choose to cultivate confidence and faith that healing can happen in my soul tribes and communities.

398 I am a role model, taking spiritual responsibility for myself to help my soul tribes and communities mature and evolve.

399 Karmic healing and spiritual blessings are here to release you from outmoded connections so that you are open to new and deeper bonds with peace in your heart.

Your guardian angel is always loving you, never judging you, always here for you, guiding and protecting you, so lean in and take shelter beneath their wings. **400**

401 My determination and persistence ensure a breakthrough, and a beautiful new day awaits!

I am capable of embodying my full soul presence. **402**

403 I ground my spirit into my body, express wisdom and evoke healing in myself and for the benefit of others.

404 The Universe knows what I need to develop strong inner foundations for future manifestations.

405 In the face of uncertainty and change, I ask Spirit to support me from within, trusting that all that is needed is always provided.

406 I open my heart to the reality of my physical existence, choosing to enter my body as I would a mysterious temple for the soul, a holder of precious teachings and blessings.

I act on and ground my intuition with practical steps, thereby helping the Universe to help me.

My gratitude for my amazing body and the many blessings in my physical world attracts further blessing and wellbeing.

I unite body, spirit and the love in my heart to infuse spiritual presence into my physical life.

I choose to never, ever give up on what truly matters to my heart.

My perseverance and determination to succeed overcomes any obstacle and opens new doorways to success.

I choose commitment in my relationships, and new healing experiences open for all. **412**

 I choose commitment in my soul groups and communities, and attain a new level of personal and spiritual empowerment that benefits all.

I align my life with my deepest truths and highest purpose. **414**

415 I live courageously, with freedom and trust.

416 I persist with confidence, constantly aligning my life with my heart.

417 I courageously continue with my healing journey, knowing that in time, it will come to fruition and bring great blessings.

418 I trust in the goodness of all that is destined for me.

419

Spiritual grace can revitalise and transform all situations and circumstances in my life.

420

My actions are worthy, so I surrender my attachment to outcomes, trusting my efforts will bear fruit, in the perfect way and at the perfect time.

421

I respect myself by choosing to invest my energies in circumstances and connections that have true value to my soul.

422

I acknowledge that my spiritual success is inevitable and act with determination, commitment, trust and restfulness.

423

I invest my energies in situations and connections that create benefits for all involved, including myself.

424

Your guardian angel brings the message that spiritual assistance is helping you heal and resolve whatever matter is now on your mind.

425

I facilitate swifter healing change by allowing others to help me.

426

I allow my heart to love with complete freedom and deep devotion.

427 The Universe sustains my healing and growth.

428 The Universe provides me with all I need to discover my inner talents and fulfil my spiritual potential.

429 My spiritual practices strengthen my connection to myself and the Universal Heart.

430 From discipline and commitment, a beautiful new reality shall be born, so attend to your process and keep the faith.

431 I trust in the inevitable transformation of effort into soul-infused manifestation.

432 The Universe provides sacred connections and opportunities to benefit my life path, at the perfect time and in the perfect way.

433 Here is your message that success will come, and you must not give up.

434 Angels are helping you co-create your life path by enhancing your connections with others and encouraging you to reach out and play.

If you are facing an obstacle or closed door, call upon the angels and your team of unconditionally loving spiritual guides, and you shall be shown a way through.

My guardian angel communicates life guidance and playful, loving messages through my heart, to reassure me that no matter what appears to be, all is well.

 My guardian angel helps me bring healing into communities that are in need, according to a higher spiritual plan.

Mother Earth knows how to help my messages of love and healing reach those in need of such wisdom.

As I commit myself to a task, my attainment is assured.

A message from the angels: "We have been sent by divine love to secure and protect your spiritual path from negative interference, and we are with you now."

 The angels say YES to the new approach, structure or foundation being created to make your dreams reality.

Divine wisdom ensures that the right people meet each other at the right time, no matter what our human perspective on such matters may be.

443 Divine will flawlessly guides me to communities that can benefit from my presence and will encourage me to grow further.

Angelic intervention is assured, and all will be well. 444

445 Behind the unexpected or unsettling events of my life, a larger, loving Divine plan is always unfolding.

As I walk my authentic path, all wants and needs are provided for by the Universe. 446

When I have a question or issue to resolve, I need only ask my guardian angel, from my heart, and the answer and the healing pathway will be revealed.

My perseverance and determination to manifest my innermost desires attract blessings and support from the Universe.

 I ask for angelic protection for me and all beings so the compassionate and loving higher plan may manifest fully with grace.

My inner spiritual foundation is strong enough to respond to change with a flexible and trusting attitude.

I allow unexpected events to inspire
flexible, creative responsiveness.

Even unexpected change benefits me and
my relationships.

 I trust that everything is going to come
together at the best time and in the best
possible way.

I relax in the knowledge that after change
and upheaval, my life is settling into a
beautiful new order.

455 I have cultivated an inner spiritual foundation of trust, strong enough to accept even the most challenging or unexpected developments with faith that it will all work out.

I experience rapid acceleration on my spiritual journey as I trust my heart. **456**

457 I trust my instincts to show me how to navigate change successfully and lovingly.

I allow my soul to guide me through challenging or confusing times with serenity and patience, knowing all is unfolding for a loving higher purpose. **458**

459 I detach from the need to control my life and surrender
into the uncertainty of change with complete trust in
the spiritual grace that is watching over me.

I allow the Universe to bless, heal and
inspire my love life.

460

461 I choose to acknowledge and enjoy my
unique and divine beauty.

I choose to acknowledge and enjoy
the divine beauty in those around me,
recognising my divine beauty, too.

462

463

I am capable of creating and sharing divine beauty to heal others and bring more joyful aliveness to the world.

As my guardian angel helps me heal my heart from past patterns, I become more able to love freely and bravely, just as my heart wishes.

I embrace changes in my love life with trust in the divine healing purpose behind all circumstances.

 I prioritise my physical and emotional wellbeing with loving self-care.

I tend to my healing journey by setting aside time to tune into my heart.

468 I take time to replenish my inner resources with self-care and time on my own.

469 I awaken a fresh chapter of love, healing and commitment in my life.

470 I am open to perspectives and philosophies that will broaden my inner and outer horizons.

471 Act on the insights and intuitions you are sensing, as they will lead you further along your authentic life path.

472 As I act on information and teachings that resonate for me, I activate my healing process.

473 I connect with like-minded communities to foster healing energies that truly nourish mind, body and soul.

474 Allow your intuition to be the deciding factor in your life decisions.

475 Have the courage to expand your religious or spiritual beliefs, to become freer and more inspired.

476 Your heart is ready for and capable of deep healing.

The time is right for my leap of faith. **477**

478 I trust my intuitive sense of timing.

I trust in endings that are essential gateways for beautiful new realities. **479**

480 I have enough inner spiritual power to handle whatever comes my way.

I believe in myself. **481**

482 I acknowledge that every person is on a unique life journey and has the free will to choose how they respond to their experiences.

I recognise that all communities have their own collective soul journey, and each individual contributes to the collective as they so choose, according to their free will. **483**

484 In creating respectful sacred space and patiently listening to my heart, I create a healing pathway from the past into the future.

485 The Universe responds with wisdom to help me remain conscious and empowered in my dealings with authority figures.

486 The wisdom and light in my heart will always prevail.

487 The Universe is actively bringing goodness and good fortune into my life.

488 I prepare myself for success, as though all that I dream of has already come to pass, and I feel gratitude, peace and confidence in the generosity and goodness of the Universe.

The Universe is actively stimulating karmic healing in my life so that I may find inner peace. **489**

490 I surrender my concerns to the Universe and allow all matters in my life to be resolved and realigned according to a higher plan.

Trust the impetus to follow new directions, as they are divinely inspired and will be part of how you fulfil your life purpose. **491**

492 I let go of toxic relationship patterns and treat myself with respect.

493 I peacefully leave behind communities that no longer serve my soul growth, with gratitude for all they have offered.

494 I peacefully leave behind old habits and lifestyle choices that no longer resonate with my soul journey, with gratitude for all I have learned.

495 I allow my past to be released, with forgiveness in my heart, so my life journey may become more vitalised and fulfilling.

496 I choose to make peace in my heart with all that has been, knowing I have become wiser and stronger, kinder and more aware through my life experiences.

497 I surrender old ways of fear and distrust and open myself to the Universe as a loving, creative partner and friend, always helping and blessing my soul.

498 I choose not to allow another to have power over my ability to love, respect and accept myself and my journey.

499 I rise from the ashes of my past, like a beautiful mythic phoenix, renewed and empowered to begin again.

When I don't understand why things are happening the way that they are, I choose to trust in the loving wisdom of the plan for my life.

I trust in the higher plan destined for me.

I trust in the higher plan destined for my relationships.

I trust in the higher plan destined for my soul tribes.

My life purpose involves choosing personal and spiritual freedom.

I allow the Universe to stimulate change in my life, evoking breakthroughs that bring freedom and relief to all areas of my life.

Higher workings of the Universe are bringing about a positive change of heart.

Higher workings of the Universe are stimulating a helpful, healing jolt of intuition to show me the best way forward.

Positive developments and changes are leading me toward greater personal and spiritual empowerment.

I open myself to a deepening change in my relationship with Spirit.

I allow the Universe to direct my course, with trust in the higher loving plan for my life.

As the creative chaos of accelerated evolution flows through my life, I stay connected to the serene truth within that reassures me everything is going to be okay.

I transcend conflict between my needs and the needs of others in relationship, connecting with the wisdom that what truly serves one soul, serves all souls equally.

I transcend conflict between my needs and the needs of others in my tribe, connecting with the wisdom that what truly serves one soul, serves all souls equally.

 I transcend any conflict between my life choices and the expectations of others, connecting with the truth that when I follow my true soul path, all beings benefit.

I choose to trust that an alchemical clash between what has been and what must be is allowing a new way to be born.

516 The Universe is always at play in my life, disrupting ego so I can connect to my heart and find true peace, happiness and spiritual fulfilment.

517 The Universe works lovingly toward my healing and my expanding wisdom, so my soul can thrive, always.

518 The Universe wants me to realise my potential and leads me to that which will help me grow into my fulfilment.

519 Instead of attempting to control, I choose to surrender and trust in the realignment that is unfolding in my life according to a mysterious and trustworthy grace.

520 I accept the unexpected as a spiritual gift.

Sacred partnerships create opportunities for my authentic self to be free from oppression and open to expression. **521**

522 I trust in the unexpected twists and turns of destiny that ensure my authentic life purpose comes to fruition.

Seemingly random meetings and connections stimulate ideas that hold the seeds of divine success. **523**

524

Unexpected partnerships that accelerate my growth and fulfilment manifest at the perfect time and in the perfect way.

Breakthroughs, opportunities and sudden
shifts take place in swift succession, stimulated
by the right people at the right time.

I open my heart and mind to a healing
breakthrough in my journey of love.

 It is safe for me to trust the spiritual intervention in
my life and I remain open to healing breakthroughs in
my relationship with my spiritual guides and higher self.

Through gratitude, I evoke the powerful blessings of the
Universal Heart, amplifying the grace and abundance
that flows into my life and through me into the world.

When relationship patterns shift at a deep spiritual level, I remain strong as any resistance resolves into karmic healing.

I am grateful for the unexpected shift into a new era of material wellbeing and spiritual blessing.

The changes sweeping through my life are clearing the way for new manifestations.

I allow others the freedom to choose how they live without judgement from me, and I give myself the same respect and courtesy.

533 My spiritual guidance and higher self reassure me that all is well, now.

I allow my plans to fall away so a higher plan can manifest itself. **534**

535 I allow Spirit to flow through my life, destabilising what is not helpful to my soul and creating a new order that will support true happiness and spiritual fulfilment.

I allow the creative intelligence of my heart to deflect and attract energies and opportunities according to what will truly empower my soul journey. **536**

537 My higher self is always loving, wise and empowered, attracting the best situations and connections, so my soul can grow into its full divine expression.

As I trust in the wisdom of divine timing, the pathway to empowerment and manifestation **538** opens for me for the greater good of all.

539 I acknowledge that new life requires the letting go of what has been, so I do this with forgiveness, curiosity and optimism for what is next to come.

Uncertainties are opportunities to anchor to a stronger inner spiritual foundation and discover what it feels like to **540** be secure within myself, no matter what happens in my life.

As previous forms, structures, attitudes and behaviours fall apart, new ways of being that are more authentic and supportive emerge.

My path of ascension requires me to relate to myself, others and the Universe with increasing love, respect and boundaries that enable my soul to thrive.

 A powerful, creative awakening is stirring within my soul, bringing the promise of new pathways and fulfilling manifestations.

The angels are guiding you to accept the changes taking place in your life and to trust that divine order is evoking realignment for your greatest fulfilment.

545 One change leads to another, triggering an
alchemical transformation of body and life
so a new self and a new way can be born.

I choose to respond to every test of my faith by further
opening my heart and becoming a vessel of divine love, a
true emanation of divine light and healing in this world.

546

547 My intuition tells me all I need to know
about how to navigate and resolve any issue
in my life.

I have the inner wisdom to deal effectively
with any upheavals and unexpected changes
in my life.

548

549 I let go of worry and concern, and trust that Spirit supports me in all areas of my life.

I embrace change, knowing it is divinely inspired and that I am inwardly equipped to accomplish a loving higher purpose. **550**

551 I fearlessly release the past and free myself through self-loving choices.

I trust in the arrival and development of the divinely destined relationships that form an integral part of my soul journey. **552**

553 I trust in the divinely destined connections and soul groups that form an integral part of my journey.

I trust the preordained twists and turns that are destined to change the course of my journey for the greater good of myself and others. **554**

555 I remain steady through any inner or outer turbulence needed to release and heal long-term issues.

I trust in the predestined twists and turns that awaken my heart and help me acknowledge my inner worth. **556**

557 I trust in the predestined twists and turns of my path that empower me to share my light with the world.

Unexpected situations reveal my inner power and creative resourcefulness so I can attract all I want and need. **558**

559 In surprising circumstances, I discover and rely upon my spiritual connection to the Universe and naturally attract an abundance of grace and protection.

I trust that the good fortune, fame, beauty and love that are meant to be part of my soul journey to help me fulfil my spiritual mission will unfold according to divine grace. **560**

561 A spontaneous shift in my connection to my heart opens my life to an inflow of fresh blessings.

562 With compassion and patience, I challenge unhelpful beliefs about relationships and open to a more loving, nourishing experience.

563 With compassion and patience, I challenge unhelpful beliefs about soul tribes, creativity and connection and open to a more loving, nourishing experience.

564 With compassion and patience, I challenge unhelpful beliefs about my body and physical health and open to a more loving, nourishing experience.

As I release belief systems that do not resonate with love, I allow healing breakthroughs and positive change to manifest in my life.

My heart is capable of healing any issue, including those of self-worth, so I can effortlessly attract all I want and need to fulfil my divine destiny.

 I allow startling insights to break through established belief systems and flow through my heart and into the world.

I release any fear of having too much by understanding the more I receive, the more that can flow through me as an offering to the greatest good for all.

With compassion and patience, I challenge unhelpful beliefs about the Divine, Spirit, religion and spirituality, to open to a more loving, nourishing experience.

The Universe supports my leaps of faith.

 With courage, I act boldly upon my intuition and break free from self-imposed limitations.

I dare to trust my instincts, act spontaneously, and share my spiritual journey as feels appropriate.

573 I take a chance and express myself creatively, spontaneously, instinctively and intuitively.

I boldly explore and heal my physical wellbeing. **574**

575 I allow my intuitive insights to inspire me to move and live in new and spontaneous ways.

I dare to explore and experience emotional freedom and psychological healing. **576**

577 I surrender ego and channel higher truths.

Everything in my life is aligning beautifully through happenings beyond my control and my spontaneous intuition. **578**

579 With gratitude and forgiveness, I release spiritual, religious or other beliefs that need to give way to new understandings arising on my soul journey.

I dethrone negative power brokers and crown my beautiful heart as the benevolent ruler of my life.

581 Negative power structures are breaking down to allow for a wiser and more loving approach to life.

As I tune into my heart, the dynamics in my relationships shift towards wisdom and love. **582**

583 I destabilise repressive ways of being to allow creative approaches to emerge.

The upheaval of changing power dynamics shall swiftly settle and ground into a new and improved way of life. **584**

585 I empower a loving change in the status quo.

I choose love over power and live with kindness and mercy toward myself and others while honouring respectful boundaries for my mind, body and soul. **586**

587 The wise choices I make based on my inner knowing, free me from struggle.

Generous blessings in all areas of my life are triggering a process of healing, transformation and fulfilment. **588**

As I surrender into wisdom and let go of power and control, my beautiful future is unfolding according to a higher loving plan.

I accept inevitable endings, letting go with peace in my heart, trusting in divine timing and the goodness of what is meant to be.

I courageously confront the darkness and discover that I hold the healing power of light within, and settle my heart and mind completely and safely in that light.

A karmic relationship pattern ends and allows me to see things with newfound clarity and peace of mind.

I give up negative beliefs about being human,
recognising I am free to live a creative, spiritual life
that contributes genuinely and positively to the planet.

Longstanding issues are now subject to spiritual
intervention for healing and new order.

No problem, confusion or difficulty can withstand
the liberating clarity and healing influence of spiritual
grace, which brings sweet relief to my life, now.

In listening to my heart and following the
spiritual guidance I find within, my life
transforms in beautiful ways.

In letting go of my attachment to chaos, confusion and criticism, I constructively and effortlessly settle into my natural state of inner freedom and spiritual light.

I give myself complete permission to debunk negative conditioning and embrace a self-view and lifestyle grounded in divine kindness, wisdom and compassion.

 Through unconditional love, I give Spirit permission to bring blessings and evoke transformation in my life, so that I may fulfil my sacred inner destiny.

I recognise that my heart belongs to the Universe, and love, abundance and countless divine blessings are bestowed on me freely.

It is my divine destiny to experience a fresh chapter of love and abundance.

 I acknowledge the twin flame and soulmate connections that are intended to heal and awaken my heart.

 As I tune into my heart and sense my connection to the Universe, I create positive energy and amplify happiness.

 My divine destiny is to manifest a successful life by living from my heart.

I open my heart to a divinely decreed breakthrough in matters of love, money and self-worth.

As I align my heart to the heart of the Universe, all manner of miraculous magic uplifts me.

 As I tune into my natural channelling abilities, I attract abundance into my life in all ways.

Earth Mother has given me the innate ability to attract all that I want and need through the magnetic power of my heart.

609

I now open my heart to
receive a profound blessing
of life-changing grace.

The Universe is guiding me through the inner knowing of my heart.

I tune into my heart and recalibrate my frequency to peace, trust and confidence in what is unfolding in my life.

I act on the urgings of my heart to initiate connections and bring creative ideas forward, and doorways open to my sacred soul destiny.

I honour the creative urgings of my heart, thus empowering myself to live my unique journey.

614 My heart knows the way.

615 I have grown strong enough to address what I have avoided in the past and can now overcome it with love and gain greater trust in my authentic self.

616 Through the power of clear intention, I graciously attract material abundance and support for my emotional wellbeing.

617 My heartfelt intentions open new channels for receiving blessings, support and assistance from the Universe.

618 I choose to honour and respect my heart.

619 I choose to commit to my soul journey without giving up.

620 My divine destiny is to experience great and passionate love in this lifetime.

 621 I am open to new ways of experiencing, expressing and demonstrating what is within my heart.

I attract heart-centred partnerships that support and are nourished by my life journey.

The love within my heart has the power to bring people together to create magic and healing laughter.

 I trust that some relationships are meant to be, and working through any issues as part of a heart-healing journey is the way to be free.

I am free to love whomever I choose.

626 I give my heart permission to love again.

My heart is a healing channel for divine love. **627**

628 I open my heart to the divine feminine, trusting in her grace and power.

I open my heart to Spirit and trust in the flow of love, grace and protection that follows. **629**

The Universe supports and encourages my creations of love.

Through the creative expression of my heart truths, a new way opens for me.

 By choosing to enter sacred partnerships, my life purpose manifests more readily and swiftly.

My heart is powerfully connected to all beings through a unifying spiritual frequency of love.

My heart attracts and manifests my most
beautiful life path.

My heart holds the key to loving
transformation that creates freedom in my
life and brings spiritual benefit to all beings.

I spontaneously evoke inner awakenings
as I express joy, love and playfulness in my
connections with others.

My heart is the wisdom key to creating
high-frequency, joyful manifestation that
amplifies abundance and healing.

There is a rightful place in this world for
my unique voice.

My heart is receptive to creations that are
truly sourced from Spirit.

My heart recognises the workings of the divine
plan, and as I awaken my heart, my life path
effortlessly unfolds in harmony with the Universe.

As I prioritise my inner life, my outer life
takes shape according to greater wisdom.

Sharing my heart truths with others is a
key facet of my life path and divine destiny.

My heart truths attract the right people at
the right time.

 My heart understands the language,
guidance and signs of the angels.

Angels speak through my heart, leading me
from darkness to light.

The Universal Heart constantly expresses loving guidance, protection and support through my heart, to support the divine destiny of all beings.

I tap into a healing channel of love, abundance and positive energy to manifest all my wants and needs.

 I am willing to honour my heart journey wherever it may lead, with confidence in the wisdom that governs my spiritual unfoldment.

Spirit provides all that is needed to manifest the beautiful aspirations shining within my heart.

As my heart wisdom grows stronger, I become free to live as my authentic self, validated from within.

 Changes in my life unfold according to a loving grace that is constantly aligning me to my inner truth and divine place in this world.

 Fluctuations and tensions in my relationships are healing transitions, which I navigate gracefully by remaining connected to my heart.

 Fluctuations and uncertainties in my soul groups and communities are healing opportunities which I navigate gracefully by remaining connected to my heart.

654 I remain connected to my heart and attract support from the Universe, so any issue with my life path, wellbeing or finances heals and transforms into abundant blessings.

655 I know all is well. I trust in the unconditional love and higher wisdom behind all that is manifesting, even the great upheavals and changes in my life.

656 I open my heart to a breakthrough in matters of love, prosperity and abundance in all ways so that my increased joy may flow into this world for the greater good.

657 I keep my heart open to the powerful magnetic quality of hope, attracting blessings and healing change to my life.

My heart attracts and guides me to my rightful place in this world to fulfil my sacred soul purpose, for the greater good of all beings.

I trust in love's greater wisdom and surrender my need to control.

 I look for the divine love that exists deep within all beings and leave all else to the Universe to resolve.

By patiently honouring the sacred wisdom of cycles and growth, every opportunity for manifesting my soul path enters my world at the best time.

Certain connections are predestined and shall manifest according to a higher plan at the time that best allows you to fulfil your spiritual journey together.

Certain relationships are predestined and shall manifest to birth creative endeavours that inspire breakthroughs in healing the human heart.

 Allow your heart to feel connected to life, remember that it is safe to trust where life leads you, and you shall be sustained and nourished by what transpires in your journey.

No matter what appears to be at this moment, have patience, for a loving destiny is unfolding in your soul and your life is taking shape to reflect that beautiful inner reality.

I gratefully receive triple blessings for abundance and heart-healing across three levels of existence—material, emotional and spiritual—for the greatest good of all.

I open my channel to the healing grace that flows through the Universe, to manifest blessings of material and spiritual wellbeing for all in need.

 The Divine Mother loves me as her own, and I am safe in her care.

I let go of any painful attachment to what has or has not been, knowing I am worthy of spiritual grace and I am open to receiving it.

670 I trust that my heart knows how to heal and is in the process of creating a new inner reality that will be expressed and grounded in the physical world.

My heart leads me to beautiful new realities that my conscious mind is yet to recognise, so I surrender my need to know right now and trust in the deeper process of loving creation. **671**

672 I effortlessly attract those who can be helped and healed by knowing me, as well as those who can help and bring healing to me.

I contribute my unique healing energies to my soul tribe, making a difference in the quality of consciousness that we co-create as a community. **673**

As I heal through my heart journey, I experience fulfilment, become what I am seeking, and integrate my material existence with my inner spiritual path.

I open my heart and mind to feel and envision complete healing, resolution and freedom in any matter of concern.

 I lovingly send the energies flowing through my heart to any situation that needs healing, with trust that the Universe supports unconditional healing.

I channel healing energies for the benefit of all beings, and my heart awakens at a deeper level of loving unity with the Universe. 677

678

The ancient priestesses of wisdom speak to my soul to empower me to continue on my path, and I gain strength from their patience, encouragement and support.

679

My heart attracts the spiritual resources needed to heal any issues in my life and contributes to healing the difficulties in this world.

680

My heart has the power to attract all I want and need, so I relax into this knowledge and enjoy the gift of life.

681

Within me are the spiritual resources needed to begin afresh, whenever I need to have hope, peace and trust in my heart.

My heart holds the inner resources of love, courage and forgiveness so my relationships can become sources of goodness, life and encouragement for myself and others.

My heart holds frequencies powerful enough to change my reality.

 Earth Mother's wild and unpredictable grace flows through my life, providing resources and lessons to help me lovingly awaken to life-enhancing spiritual truths.

The magnetic field of my heart holds the power to reshape my reality.

My heart holds wisdom that the logical mind
cannot comprehend, so I choose to trust my heart,
irrespective of whether it makes sense at the time.

I seek the healing wisdom of the heart that is
never constrained by what the mind thinks it
knows, and in doing so, I awaken and heal.

The desires of my heart are in
harmony with the greater plan the
Universe holds for me.

As I pray authentically from the heart, Earth
Mother and Great Spirit respond together,
manifesting the grace needed to heal our world.

690 I gracefully surrender what has been, with love, forgiveness and trust in my heart, clearing the way for a blessed new reality to emerge.

I lovingly bring my involvement in situations not aligned with my inner spiritual truth to an end, whenever I choose. **691**

 692 I lovingly release my attachment to certain people, allowing Spirit to show me when further work is needed and when our spiritual contract is fulfilled.

I gain closure by making peace in my heart about my past involvement in groups and communities, acknowledging that I have become wiser through my experiences. **693**

I am guided to release attachment, judgement or concern about an issue in my life, allowing my heart to relax and receive a healing blessing of completion from Spirit.

When I let go from deep within my heart, healing change and freedom will come.

 My heart holds the spiritual intelligence to distil wisdom from every experience so that I am always growing stronger, more open, luminous and boldly loving.

I trust my intuition to show me when a situation is naturally drawing to a close, and I let go to allow for a new and loving reality of healing to manifest.

698 I love and respect my body as a unique and extraordinary companion that allows my Spirit to manifest this wisdom-creating gift of human life.

In every ending, small and great, there is spiritual grace, offering shelter, love and healing. **699**

700 Your higher self knows what is happening and how to move through it, even when your conscious mind does not, so trust your higher self and know you are going to be okay.

When you act from your higher self, you won't always understand why you are doing what you are doing, but it will always feel loving, right and somehow aligned with Spirit. **701**

702

Spirit is always with you,
and you are never alone.

703 Your higher self lovingly encourages you to approach life with a happy attitude, which will clear unnecessary suffering.

704 I trust my intuition to reveal the divine plan for my life, at the best time and in the best way.

705 Put your faith in what you sense is on the way but may not yet be evident in your outer world.

706 Your higher self encourages you to rely upon your sense of humour to soften your concerns and attract better solutions, especially regarding seemingly serious matters.

707 I can ask any question from the Universe and will receive an answer, for as I seek, so shall I find.

My intuition wisely guides my expressions of power, leadership and influence. **708**

709 I tune into my deep spiritual connection to the Universe, naturally channelling energy that supports release, healing and renewal.

Trust in the pathways opening up for you. **710**

711
There is a star seed of higher consciousness within my soul, reminding me to believe in and be my true self, always.

712
I set my intention to create healing outcomes in my relationships, and attract supporting insights, connections and information.

713
I surrender the belief that I have to be a lone wolf, and my choice to connect with others awakens playful and vitalising energies.

714
My clear intentions cause energy to flow in the best directions for healing and manifestation.

715 The spiritual power to change and heal my life is within me.

716 The spiritual power to heal and empower my heart is within me.

717 My intention to heal sets my recovery in motion, and as I listen for and follow the signs that resonate with me, I take the healing journey that sets me free.

718 The loving power of destiny guides me forward at all times.

719 I put my faith in the healing power of Spirit to bring all situations into balance and restoration in accord with higher loving wisdom.

The Universe brings me into connection with the right people at the right time, according to a loving plan that holds spiritual blessings for all. **720**

721 I remain emotionally intimate with others while remaining authentic in my inner truth.

I trust my intuitive sense of higher purpose and the deeper meaning of my life. **722**

723

As I trustingly open to my higher self, I attract all that is needed to bring my inner visions to life.

724

My higher self is practical and attracts all the material resources needed to manifest my soul purpose.

725

My higher self knows what is happening in my life and how to successfully find the way through any challenge, even when my conscious mind doesn't know it is safe to trust.

726

As I tune into my heart, I can feel the loving spiritual guidance of my higher self.

727 As I tune into my higher self, I am able to channel healing energy into my relationships, surrendering attachment to how I think things should go and allowing love to lead the way.

728 My higher self has the spiritual capacity to disentangle relationship difficulties, to help me to grow in wisdom and bring out the best in me.

729 My higher self attracts sacred partnerships that will help me heal and manifest my divine life purpose.

730 My higher self is a creative healer. It bears tremendous spiritual resources and is capable of transforming any struggle into joyful freedom.

731 My higher self can more easily inspire me with guidance when I balance discipline with relaxation and play.

732 When I am playful with others, I increase creative energies within myself and them.

733 The conscious embrace of my spiritual healing journey grows the light in this world and supports the awakening of many humans.

734 Sacred play creates a field of high-frequency energy, attracting the opportunities I need to manifest my destiny.

735 Sacred play creates new perspectives and positively shakes things up to bring freedom to my heart.

736 I connect to my higher self through my heart and tap into a wellspring of creativity, healing and infinite inner resources.

737 I am my higher self and reach new levels of inspired manifestation by attracting creative connections.

738 By honouring my creative and spiritual journey, I attract good fortune and special blessings.

739

As I heal myself, I learn to use my sensitivity as a strength, making my special connection to the loving realm of Spirit more conscious and helpful than ever.

My intuition flawlessly guides me through all material concerns and attracts divine support for my life path.

740

741

I sense and implement a new plan which leads me to success.

I trust my intuition and choose to partner with truly supportive allies.

742

743 I align myself with conscious communities and soul groups that support and benefit from my creative self-expression.

744 My intuition senses the presence of angels and reminds me that when I ask for help sincerely, divine assistance is always given.

745 I intuitively understand how to create healing change in my life.

746 I honour my intuition and act on what moves my heart, generating beautiful opportunities for future success.

747
By tuning into my higher self and acting on my inner guidance, I am ascending to an entirely new frequency of consciousness.

748
I trust in the divine power of Earth Mother, as she actively works toward the spiritual fulfilment of all beings - including me!

749
Spiritual practices such as yoga, meditation, prayer, therapy, dream journaling and personal reflection empower my progress and awaken divine connections.

750
The changes the Universe brings into my life are for a loving higher purpose.

751

I choose to be influenced by what truly inspires me, and so I unplug from sources of negativity, within me or around me, that drain and diminish my vital life force.

752

Self-restricting, long-term patterns of relating are now healing from within.

753

I allow my intellectual, logical mind to take comfort in and surrender to the greater wisdom of my intuitive understanding.

754

I take practical steps to implement positive changes in my life, and this will result in healing.

755 I am willing to sacrifice a need for certainty and control so greater healing, happiness and freedom can occur.

Things are going to come together, and you are going to have a positive change of heart. **756**

757 As I trust my inner knowing unconditionally and allow it to guide me, no matter where it appears to lead, I swiftly attain higher levels of success.

I trust in the higher purpose of my talents, knowing they are meant to be expressed, and that even when I don't understand how, they are healing and helpful to others. **758**

759 My inner healing journey opens new horizons for me, internally and in my physical world.

760 I tune into the reassuring voice of my heart that lets me know I am going to be okay, even when I don't understand how.

761 I don't always understand why something is happening, but I can still benefit from it by tuning into my higher self and trusting I will be guided through it.

762 I honour and respect my heart's need to feel and be connected.

763 My higher self is always guiding me from within, with wisdom, never judging or criticising me or anyone else, and only ever providing loving solutions.

My heart's guidance resolves all matters, practically and spiritually, to overcome ebbs and obstacles and bringing me to flow and success. **764**

765 I am worthy of breaking free from what has been so that I can move swiftly into a new expression.

I trust that I am worthy to receive. **766**

767 I put my trust in what I sense is unfolding, in goodness and grace, even before there is evidence of it manifesting in my world.

768 I give myself healing and love because I am worthy to receive such tender self-care.

769 I give my space for making spiritual connections and processing inner healing because I am worthy of respect and the far-reaching benefits of living this way.

770 The Universe directs my healing journey, and it is safe to trust in its wisdom, rather than trying to figure everything out in advance.

771 My inner healer is an extension of the great cosmic healer, inspiring me with what is possible when I tune into its spiritual power.

772 When I ask the Universe for unconditionally loving assistance, my healing energies are amplified.

773 I allow for synergy between my body, my mind and my heart, and they resonate harmoniously, creating a strong channel for swift healing.

774 My healing journey brings practical benefits to myself and others, even if that is not always obvious to the logical mind.

775 I give the intelligence of the Universe freedom to move through my life as it chooses, honouring its loving wisdom, as its grace always serves the greatest good.

776 I open to the healing energies of the Universe and ask that my heart be granted what it most needs to become whole and flourish for the good of all.

777 You will heal.

778 I embrace my body's healing journey with unconditional trust, knowing there is a loving purpose in what is unfolding.

779

Spirit is gifting you with
the power to heal.

780 The Universe is guiding me so I can unite my body and mind in the frequency of love.

781 Sacred feminine intelligence knows how to birth all things, including my life path, so I trust in her inspirations and feel them in my body.

782 I heal my connection to the earth and sense her as a loving mother and generous creatrix who supports my life journey.

783 I listen for Earth Mother's signs and symbols as she guides me to manifest my creative soul expression.

784 I allow my body to show me the steps to take for healing and manifestation, including when to act and when to rest.

I feel freer, more spontaneous and more peaceful in the event of change when I anchor my security in **785** a loving connection with my spirit and my body.

786 I heal my connection to my body by learning to love and appreciate the wonderful natural powers of creation, attraction, healing and expression it holds.

I discern and trust the wisdom messages of my body, and it leads me to wellbeing. **787**

788 My journey involves mastery and success
on spiritual and material levels.

My higher self guides me into my destiny as a light
bearer on this planet, one who holds a frequency of
unconditional love for the benefit of all beings. **789**

790 I choose to trust Spirit.

I trust in what inspires me. **791**

792 I give up my sense of isolation, recognising that Spirit is with me, lovingly and always.

I surrender any belief that I need to figure everything out on my own and open my heart to the loving input of Spirit to create better outcomes for all. **793**

794 I allow my body to become an instrument through which the spiritual grace of life creatively expresses itself, rather than treating it as a project to be perfected.

I unconditionally trust in the spiritual grace that enables even the most difficult karma to transform into a blessing for which I am truly grateful. **795**

796 I ask Spirit to heal my heart and free me from past struggles so I may open to the greater experience intended for me.

I surrender my concerns into the healing frequency of Spirit, through which liberation is enabled, and the ways to transcend old patterns are mastered. **797**

798 Spirit flows through me, unimpeded, manifesting grace in this world.

In every ending, a secret grace manifests and leads me into deeper joy, spirituality and fulfilment. **799**

I receive divine blessings for complete fulfilment and the manifestation of my soul purpose.

I tune into my courage, take my journey and continue to manifest my sacred life path.

Predestined karmic connections enter my life and awaken a new phase of manifestation, blessing and empowerment, according to divine timing.

A new era is dawning for me.

804 My life is taking shape according to a higher plan of divine destiny.

What appears to be unexpected or uncertain is not so, but rather has been orchestrated at the spiritual level to ensure the fulfilment of your soul path.

805

806 I open my heart to the liberating divine power of forgiveness.

I tune into my inner knowing, and in applying what I find within, I am empowered to manifest spiritual beauty in this world.

807

The divine feminine empowers and shelters me within her protection, wisdom and far-reaching influence.

You'll know when it is the right time for your leap of faith.

 I exercise my power of choice by taking action that is inspired by love, from a place of patience and wisdom, with an excellent sense of timing.

I boldly choose to feel, believe in and embody the higher-level frequencies I wish to manifest in my life and the world.

812

I empower myself and accelerate my spiritual development by initiating sacred partnerships.

813

I have the creative energy necessary to bring life, vitality and playfulness into my soul groups and communities.

814

I choose to lead by example, growing into my spiritual maturity and opening a pathway for others to grow with me.

I lead by giving others the freedom to embody their authentic soul journey.

815

816 I lead from the heart and empower others to connect with themselves.

817 I lead intuitively, encouraging others to discover their own inner truths.

818 Earth Mother encourages me to embrace my role as a leader by tuning into greater wisdom than my own, so I may lead in a way that serves all.

819 I commit to my spiritual journey, even when it takes me away from what I have known.

820 I recognise the Universe as my sacred partner in co-creation, and lean into Source, relaxed in the knowledge that everything is coming together.

As I balance intimacy with others and the solitude which provides intimacy with myself and Spirit, my capacity for manifestation is radically amplified.

821

822 There is a unique place and purpose in this world that only I can fulfil.

I connect to the sacred feminine energies to create a safe healing space for my authentic self-expression.

823

I invite the angelic healing of unconditional love into all areas of my spiritual, psychological, emotional and physical life, now.

I increase my sphere of influence by living from my heart.

 I open and align my heart with the Divine, unconditionally trusting in the goodness and grace intended for me.

As I connect my inner channel to Spirit, I increase the sphere of loving influence in this world.

I align myself with the path intended for me by the Universe and surrender into what is, so that what must be, can be.

In surrendering to the wise will of Spirit, I gain access to unlimited resources so I can manifest my destiny for the greatest good of all.

 Earth Mother generously provides creative resources to support my spiritual journey, and in gratitude, I dedicate my journey to bringing peace and healing to this planet.

A new chapter in creativity and self-expression is awakening in my life, as arranged at a spiritual level to ensure the continued blossoming of my soul.

832 I recognise Earth Mother as a loving, creative, resourceful soul friend, who supports me with all I need to manifest my soul destiny for the good of all beings.

I now ask for assistance from the unconditionally loving spiritual guides that help with all earthly matters, so the divine plan may manifest fully and freely. **833**

834 I make a caring, creative offering to Mother Nature's earth angels in gratitude for their powerful assistance, protection and healing in my life.

I patiently listen to Earth Mother for signs of where I can send healing to help create positive change, as an act of gratitude for her generous gifts in my life. **835**

I lovingly share the stories of my life journey so others may find comfort, reassurance and peace.

I share uplifting intuitions and playfulness with others so that they may find healing and trust in their journey.

I allow my voice to be heard.

I am open about my spiritual journey so others may gain a sense that they, too, are free to explore and commit to their own unique path.

I am spiritually empowered to lead others in this lifetime, and I choose to do so with compassion and spiritual responsibility.

I boldly take steps to lovingly shine my light as a spiritual leader on this planet, encouraging others to live their lives fully and freely, by embodying trust, peace and playfulness.

Earth Mother is my friend and guide, and I trust in her plan for me.

It is part of my life journey that I grow, evolve into my true self and feel more like myself than ever before.

844
I call upon loving angels to guide me, so that my life may faithfully reflect, and be sheltered within, the greater divine plan.

845
Predestined yet seemingly sudden shifts, destabilise long-held conditions and bring greater joy and freedom to my life.

846
Divine love shall rock my world, and it is safe to let it happen.

847
An important truth shall be revealed, and your world will reshape itself in harmony with your highest purpose.

848 I focus on grounding, connecting to my body and the earth, so that the sacred partnership between heaven and earth may manifest itself in my life.

I have the good fortune to be able to focus and empower my spiritual journey by committing to a regular spiritual practice. **849**

850 My luck is changing for the better.

Change brings a fortunate boon to your life. **851**

Sacred partnership will change your life in surprising and wonderful ways.

The sacred communities that are karmically intended for you, will help you find healing, know the freedom to be yourself, and be loved for who you are.

 Change will flow through your life like a breath of fresh air, bringing much-needed release from the past and creating a foundation to begin anew.

Rapid changes may feel unpredictable or evoke uncertainty, but they are part of the divine plan and can result in an abundant flow of love and prosperity.

856

Embrace change, for it
is leading you toward
your heart's desire.

857 A sudden intuitive insight shall unleash your personal and spiritual power.

858 My divine destiny involves a healing transformation of my body and my finances.

859 I am surrounded by a powerful field of spiritual protection, which is divinely bestowed for my life journey and cannot be overcome.

860 I am blessed to manifest the passion of my heart.

As I trust the journey of my life, the loving plan that Mother Earth has for me becomes known to my heart.

I trust in the relationships Earth Mother has intended for me so I may empower my heart and gain confidence in my intuition.

I am capable of creating, attracting and connecting with what I truly want and need.

My heart has a plan in complete harmony with the Universe, and as I follow it, I align myself with great power, protection and grace.

I follow my heart straight into the lucky twist of fate that is intended for me.

Good karma and kind choices enable me to receive an abundance of love and prosperity, which I gratefully accept and dedicate to furthering my spiritual path.

My loving exploration of spirituality opens avenues for healing and empowerment.

I bow to my heart and serve her as my inner queen.

869 Through my heart, I unite the spiritual and the earthly, honouring the sacred beauty in this world.

As I choose to respect my truth, all else falls into place. **870**

871 My actions align my life with my inner truth and open a channel for positive spiritual energy to flow into my life.

My authentic emotional intimacy with myself and with others empowers my relationships and my soul. **872**

I give myself the authority to validate my creative expression and spiritual journey.

I choose to live and act according to my truth.

 You are free to live as you choose.

My higher self creates a powerful field of attraction through my heart and draws whatever is needed to my life.

877
I accept that my path is a transformative journey through which I will become a capable channel of healing energies that bring benefit to all beings.

My higher self attracts the blessings and abundance required to fulfil my life purpose. **878**

879
An important matter is swiftly approaching resolution.

A wish shall be granted. **880**

You shall attain self-mastery on a matter of personal and spiritual significance.

You shall attain self-mastery through a relationship matter.

You shall attain self-mastery in a situation to do with community, the collective or group consciousness.

I choose to activate the law of attraction by embodying the qualities I wish to amplify in my life.

Through a lucky break, which is really a case of good karma, a stroke of good fortune enters my life.

My heart is capable of attracting luck, blessings and good fortune of all kinds.

 I trust in the power and resourcefulness of my higher self.

Here are blessings for supreme success on all levels—material, emotional, psychological and spiritual—and a message that the divine plan is manifesting beautifully in your life.

889 Divine blessings help me release the past and become free to accept an abundance of new opportunities.

890 I am most joyful, wise and effective when I surrender my opinions and align myself with the greater workings of a higher power.

891 In surrendering to a higher power, I know which steps to take, in harmony with higher wisdom and divine timing.

892 I have the ability to align with my higher self as I set an intention to connect and receive from a spiritual source of unconditional loving wisdom.

893 As I actively surrender my attachment and control to higher wisdom, I am infused with the protection of the Universe.

894 Spirit is offering to intervene in a material concern, which I accept by saying, "I invite the unconditional love, wisdom and protection of Spirit to manifest for my benefit, now."

895 I allow the Universe to usher healing changes into my life, detaching me from past problems and opening a pathway for genuine fulfilment and success.

896 I rest peacefully in the knowledge that my heart and my path are divinely protected by spiritual grace.

I am learning a spiritual lesson of great value at this time, which will soon afford me increased power, freedom and wisdom to manifest in my life in new ways.

I trust that I am an old soul, with wisdom and a nourishing spiritual connection to an infinite supply of grace and abundance.

 With wisdom, I surrender all things to the Universe.

Spirit brings a message: A cycle of divine harvest is now upon you. Good things shall emerge from your efforts.

I have a divine blessing to begin again,
with more wisdom, complete forgiveness for
myself and others and a clean spiritual slate.

I offer all my relationships to Spirit for karmic
healing so loving fulfilment may manifest for
all, according to higher wisdom and grace.

I belong to a soul group, within which I have
a spiritual role to play so that together we can
evoke healing, joy and creative freedom.

The Divine has a special plan and higher
purpose for me and my life and asks me to
trust and act in commitment to that purpose.

905

A spiritual blessing received on the inner planes suddenly initiates an unexpected change in my life, averting difficulty and enhancing grace.

Spirit loves me with great devotion and passion. All my needs shall be provided for so my life path may find fulfilment.

906

907

Spirit is guiding me toward the answers I need, and I can access those answers by tuning into my intuition.

The source of all true and genuinely great power flows from Spirit.

908

The wisdom of the ancient sages and seers can be found within my soul, so I quietly turn within and listen for their guidance.

From the fruit of past actions, new pathways are becoming available to me.

 I am going through an initiation process which is igniting rapid spiritual expansion, so I choose to trust unconditionally in what I AM becoming.

Turn your attention to the loving worlds of Spirit, and your new energies will invigorate your relationships.

From the harvest of past efforts, new seeds are stimulated, and a new era is dawning.

The Universe shall provide new resources to support your material existence and help you break through into new territory.

 Helpful twists of fate are intended for you and are being orchestrated by the loving world of Spirit so that your heart may experience freedom and peace.

A new karmic cycle, one of healing and spiritual depth, is dawning for your heart.

917 With gratitude, I accept a fresh cycle of healing that is helping me break cleanly and completely from past experiences.

You have the power to overcome the past and start anew. **918**

919 You are blessed with the power to overcome any obstacle.

The Universe is a creative ally who says YES to whatever I wish to focus my heart and mind on. **920**

921

Inspiration is coming your way to help you successfully resolve that which has concerned you, so keep your heart open, and your mind relaxed.

922

I call upon the spiritual guides who love me unconditionally for assistance and protection in all matters to do with my life journey, now.

923

I connect with Spirit, surrendering my opinions and expectations and allowing for a loving reorientation to flow into my soul, through my mind and into my life.

924

The strength of my spiritual connection gives me the determination to refuse to give up on myself.

925

I am open to
life-changing grace.

926 My heart is open to Spirit, allowing for unconditional love to fill me, changing my thoughts, healing my feelings and bringing forth a new way to proceed.

I align my inner channel with the loving realm of Spirit, understanding that all issues and concerns can be healed through spiritual intervention. **927**

928 You will be provided with the relationships you need for your healing.

I ask that past-life patterns in present-life relationships are healed through unconditional love for the greater freedom and peace of all. **929**

930

Trust your positive karma.

931

My spiritual harvest is drawing near, in accord with divine timing.

932

I attract the perfect opportunities and connections to manifest my soul vision for the greater good.

933

I unite with Spirit, and divine creations pour forth from my soul, bringing compassion and beauty into this world.

934

My spiritual connection empowers me to take practical steps to bring my visions to life in this world.

I actively pray for healing change, and in doing so, I create space for divine blessings to manifest.

935

936

I have faith in the power of prayer to create love.

I have faith in the power of prayer to create healing.

937

Positive returns on past karmic efforts are accumulating and shall empower me to manifest that which may appear miraculous to others.

The Universe encourages you to apply the effort needed to bring your creative projects and visions to completion.

 I have the positive karma needed to make a commitment to spiritual practice in this lifetime, so I can make personal progress and bring much-needed light to this planet.

Beginning or renewing a spiritual practice will change your life.

942 Creating space in your relationships for spiritual practice supports your awakening and the awakenings of your loved ones.

Your spiritual practice has far-reaching effects, bringing positive healing energies into your reality, as well as the lives of your tribes and communities. **943**

944 Your guardian angel is with you now, bringing a message that a difficult time is coming to an end and you shall be freed, healed and protected as you move into a new cycle.

The breakthrough, lucky break, good fortune and healing change you are seeking can and will come to you through committed spiritual practice.

I listen to my heart and discover a deep desire to commit to my spiritual practices as a daily renewal and source of love, comfort and joy.

I tap into a powerful inner channel of healing energies through my spiritual practice.

My spiritual practices empower me to manifest my light in this world.

In grounding myself, I embody, honour and empower my spiritual journey.

950 The more uncertainty in my life, the deeper I connect with the loving worlds of Spirit and the greater the liberation, light and creative life force that shall emerge from the chaos.

Seeds planted now shall yield good fortune and heart-centred manifestations in the future. **951**

952 I allow for unexpected changes and uncertainties in my life, realising they are part of how the Universe answers my prayers.

As I let go of what has been, I open to original, authentic expressions of spontaneous, creative solutions. **953**

954 My spiritual practices help heal and liberate others.

955 My practice of prayer is an act of free will that triggers a healing change for the greater good.

956 Through every challenge, I choose to align more closely and authentically with my heart. I thus gain spiritual power and grace to assist me in all ways.

957 A spiritual gift shall evoke healing change and bring good fortune in your life.

A positive change in your status is in line with your divine path and soul purpose.

Through the workings of karma, a series of shifts and endings shall establish a new level of freedom and fortune in your life.

Open your heart to the blessings the Universe wishes to bestow upon you.

Align your heart with the Universal Heart, and in that state of loving surrender, you shall always take the best step at the best time.

962 Allow the Universe to mirror the beauty of your heart back to you so you may feel ready, worthy and empowered to manifest your destiny.

Kindness, to oneself and others, is astonishingly powerful. **963**

964 Through grace, I am empowered to express and manifest the inner beauty of my heart in this world.

Follow your heart and be gifted with the spiritual keys for transforming your reality. **965**

966 By trusting that I can attract material abundance and prosperity, I release the grip of survival fears and deepen my loving bond with Spirit.

I am able to discern the spiritual reality beneath appearances.

 967

968 I choose to take pleasure in my spiritual practices and life journey.

Through the forgiveness of others and myself, I manifest extraordinary freedom that is a powerful and much-needed healing force in our human collective.

 969

970 My spiritual practice creates a field of healing energy that the Divine can use to bless beings through me, according to a higher plan and purpose.

Allow yourself to be recalibrated by divine grace so you may be an instrument of higher spiritual workings, even when you are not aware of it. **971**

972 A loving team of spiritual guides supports you on your healing journey. As you heal, you help the human collective to heal, too.

The ability to evoke healing through your sense of humour is part of your spiritual inheritance.

974 Grounding spiritual awareness to make the path practical and accessible for yourself and others is an ability that is part of your spiritual inheritance.

Your prayers are needed to initiate change on a spiritual level, so the Divine has permission to act in your life and in the world, to benefit to all. **975**

976 Sometimes there is nothing to be done, except to love, feel and be.

My trust in the healing journey paves the way for miracles. **977**

978 Through spiritual grace, wounded realities give way to healing, and the higher truth of the heart shall finally be recognised.

There is a wisdom greater than our limited understanding can ever comprehend, yet we can recognise that it is safe to trust in its love, surrender with peace and rest in its mysteries. **979**

980 There are times when earthly matters must give way to the spiritual workings of a higher plan, so no matter what appears to be at this time, trust in your destiny.

I tend to my inner wellbeing and replenish myself through a deep connection with my soul to empower for my spiritual evolution. **981**

I recognise the Universe as a cosmic mirror, faithfully and lovingly reflecting the abundance, love and gratitude I choose to focus upon.

Creative self-expression and playfulness can now be used as a circuit breaker for negative patterning, liberating and redirecting those energies into more constructive expressions.

In my heart, I unite the loving energies of Spirit, the sacred feminine and the angels to gain supreme spiritual blessings and the empowerment of my soul destiny.

I am destined to expand and express my loving spiritual influence across new horizons.

I rest in the depths of my heart, where I find sanctuary and the restoration needed to leave the past behind each day and begin anew in the gift of each morning.

Your spiritual practices empower you as a healer, lending healing qualities to your presence in all situations.

You reach new levels of attainment through your spiritual practices.

Your spiritual practices are gathering energy to establish positive foundations for a loving new cycle of empowerment.

990 A divine blessing is now given for the resolution and karmic completion of an old cycle.

Divine blessings are now granting a spiritually protected new chapter in your life. **991**

 992 A significant relationship is important to your soul journey and protected by divine grace.

Through playfulness, I experience karmic clearing, healing and freedom. **993**

Ask your guardian angel and unconditionally loving guides for help as you hand over what has troubled you, and a resolution shall swiftly follow.

I dare to believe in miracles and invoke them through passionate and peaceful prayer.

 I pray directly from my heart, pulling divine grace into my life and touching the lives of those I love.

My passionate prayers create space to receive healing miracles.

I surrender my will to the higher will of
Spirit and gain access to the powerful
healing grace of the Universe.

Allow the highest and most powerful
consciousness—that of true, unconditional love—to
be your protector, your guide and your friend.

I allow myself to pause and prepare for
an imminent spiritual reboot into a fresh,
inspired beginning.

I open myself to the brilliance and
inventiveness of Spirit and allow fresh
magic to weave itself through my life.

The Universe says: "I am your cosmic best friend, always holding your heart in my own, always lovingly guiding you."

The Universe says: "There are certain people you are meant to connect with to complete karmic contracts and create joyful healing outcomes."

The Universe says: "I am showing you the way to resolve all practical matters, so stay connected to your inner spirit to sense my signs and guidance now."

The Universe says: "A shift is needed to align you with the path destined for you, so there's no need to worry if things are a bit bumpy for a while."

The Universe says: "I communicate with you via your heart, so when you need to know something, tune into the deepest inner truth of your heart, and you'll find my guidance there within you."

The Universe says: "I am bringing some helpful information to your attention, so keep filtering through the distractions, until you find what resonates."

The Universe says: "You have an empowered voice, so even though it's not always easy, use your thoughts and your words to align you with the grace of Spirit.

The Universe says: "A karmic obstacle has become too entrenched for you to heal on your own, so I am providing divine intervention to help you to shift it once and for all."

The past, and all attachment to it, must give way to what is divinely meant to be.

An inspirational jolt of intuition is going to cut through your suffering, revealing a positive spiritual reality beneath the worried workings of your mind.

When relationship matters seem overly complicated, come back to the basics of giving and receiving from a place of love, honesty, respect, kindness and patience.

Stay connected to the original inspiration for your creative and community endeavours so that integrity is preserved.

1014

Your deep and authentic sense of purpose is the best foundation for your decisions, and as you align with that, the Universe can more easily support you.

1015 A life-altering event, opportunity or spontaneous happening is going to evoke healing energy for you, and your concerns shall fade away.

Expect a positive adjustment in your love life and finances. **1016**

1017 Allow the Universe to guide you, and you shall make important breakthroughs in your healing journey and significant spiritual progress.

1018 Through a divinely destined sequence of events, you shall be moved into a more prominent position with a greater reach and sphere of influence.

You are only afraid to let go because you sense the radical and rapid evolution that will happen when you do, yet it is through such change that a prayer will be answered. **1019**

1020 At a soul level, you are taking a step up the ladder of evolution, which is not always a smooth transition, but ultimately yields a positive outcome.

A divine key in the form of a spiritual gift shall be offered to you, granting the capacity to open doors previously closed to you.

Your spiritual foundations are strong enough for you to rely upon as a source of peace and support, even during the uncertainties of change.

 You are rapidly evolving from fear-based to love-based systems. If fear-based beliefs arise, consider how to compassionately heal them, rather than accepting them as a reflection of reality.

1024 As you commit to and work toward your goals, you will attract supportive helpers when needed and successfully manifest your plans. Do not allow yourself to be deterred.

The Universe will rattle psychological cages to liberate you from the controlling mindsets that would hold you back from embracing the next phase of your life journey. **1025**

1026 Karmic healing will happen as you invite change by reaching out with love.

Take the initiative in recruiting helpful allies on your path.

Align yourself with those who embody the vision and spiritual wholeness to which you aspire.

 A karmic event shall close a chapter in a relationship, evoke inner healing and create a pathway to new, more authentic connection.

Look at a situation directly, realistically, and choose to view it as an opportunity for growing your faith, rather than your fear.

As you ask the Universe for resources and positive solutions, you will find the means to transform a negative into a positive and gain spiritual strength.

Fearful belief systems take many lifetimes to develop, so be patient with yourself as you cultivate—and learn to trust in—more loving and helpful viewpoints.

The Universe will soon provide you with a spiritual gift that will help you overcome negative karma in a beautiful, heroic and inspirational way.

Harmonise your mind, body and soul with the protective energy of your loving heart so you no longer feel pulled in competing directions and can rest.

The challenges in your life are not going to hold you back; they are spiritual tests that are helping you shed your fear and become a happier person.

Your heart brings you a message that it is currently magnetising a more beautiful reality, and it asks you to keep your mind open and free from negative expectations.

Allow your intuition, rather than mass consciousness, to inspire, guide and inform your decisions.

 Dare to believe that everything is going to be okay.

1039 Your spiritual journey will sometimes lead you to confront negativity so it can heal; this is not a sign that you—or another—has done something wrong.

A way shall be found to free you from negative constraints. **1040**

1041 Whatever your judgements of a situation, you are making progress on your life path and spiritual journey and are urged not to give up or turn away from what truly matters to your heart.

1042

You cannot always know how a karmic wound with another is going to heal or how that healing will look. But as you commit to your heart journey and claim forgiveness for yourself and others, you can know that such healing will occur, and you shall both become free.

Something you never thought would heal, will do so through the workings of divine will.

1043

1044

Your earthly concerns are moving into alignment with the higher will of Spirit, and through that process, a difficult situation will be positively transformed.

1045 The precious gem of your heart has been polished and refined through challenge and is strong enough to withstand outer turmoil without wavering in its radiant creation of peace, beauty and light.

See a negative situation as a vote of confidence from the Universe and remain optimistic and confident – you have the capacity and the destiny to grow more luminous and spiritually empowered than whatever challenge you are currently facing. **1046**

1047 You shall discover new ways to approach a troubling issue, breaking the bonds that have held you hostage to old patterns and freeing up energy to make rapid progress on your path.

1048 Commit to your efforts, as you have innate talent and the ability to generate resources and attract an abundance of spiritual energy to manifest your dreams for the greater good.

1049 The miraculous operates beyond the confines, expectations and limitations of the mind and generously manifests for those willing to open their hearts with trust in the higher workings of goodness and grace.

1050 The challenges in your life will not harm you – they are helping you grow your faith and be open to more blessings in your life.

1051 Something that appears to fail or fall short of your expectations shall bring a blessing, and an improved path or approach shall become clear to you.

The Universe knows you have come to this planet to accomplish something positive. It asks you to remain flexible and optimistic, even in the face of your fear, so things can work out for the best. **1052**

1053 You probably cannot see it at the moment, but something good, healing and positive is unfolding within the depths of your being and will soon find its way into the world.

1054 Just as the tide withdraws before it flows to the shore again, you can accept temporary losses, apparent defeats, reversals and ebbs in your progress as precursors to a larger win, fresh inflow and the abundant blessing which is on its way.

1055 Every change, upheaval and uncertainty—especially those that appear negative on the surface—are part of how the Universe adjusts your path to ensure your success.

1056 When you open your heart to Spirit, even a dire or stubborn issue can be transformed in an instant, as though it simply never existed.

1057 For those who seek them, there are infinite spiritual pathways and divine resources available to resolve every problem, so tune into your spiritual connection and ask for help with the genuine belief that a solution will be provided.

There are many ways you can grow, and the Universe always provides a path to fulfilment, so it is okay to trust where you are being led and have faith that things are working out, even though it may not always seem that way. **1058**

1059 When you are connected to your heart, you have the capacity to assume numerous responsibilities and successfully organise and prioritise in a way that promotes long-term success for many.

1060

Your heart holds an accurate, positive prediction for your future which is directly received from the Universe and accessible when you calm your mind and turn within.

Taking the initiative to develop and express your talents will bring you material success and spiritual growth.

You will have the freedom to successfully manifest the work your heart yearns for, attracting supportive, beneficial helpers who champion your progress.

 Your heart has a greater capacity to generate love, abundance, connection and creative pathways than you realise.

There is an inspired solution to any problem: tune into the heart, genuinely ask for help, and the way shall be shown, so relax, reach out and trust your ability to draw a positive outcome to your world.

Assume your responsibilities with courage, knowing you have the inner strength and dignity of spirit to meet life's challenges successfully and with integrity.

Your soul has a heightened ability to influence others, and as you express that talent with kindness (without attempting to control anyone), you will dramatically increase your magnetism and personal power.

1067 You have the independence of mind, heart and soul to pursue your inner spiritual awakening, adjusting to the demands of your authentic healing journey and making swift progress towards enlightenment as you do so.

1068 You have what it takes for success, and the Universe shall provide all that is needed for you to meet your potential.

1069 Your heart can perceive the knowledge that comes from beyond the physical realm and intuitively knows how to act on it to bring about healing, growth and success in all areas of your life.

1070 Outer effort is important, but a more considerable power for bringing about change in the world flows from inner alignment with the spiritual world.

As you calm your mind and allow yourself to become emotionally neutral, you shall perceive the answer that will stem your worries, clear confusion and unveil a constructive approach for whatever matters are of concern at this time. **1071**

1072 Sharing insights with trustworthy allies will help clarify and create an inspired way to further your progress.

1073 Your dreams shall manifest.

Be unwavering in the face of challenge, knowing that your spiritual foundation is strong enough to support you and attract positive alternatives. **1074**

1075 By forcing yourself to try to understand more than you can readily grasp at this moment, you will become unnecessarily confused, so it is better to focus on the next step and trust that the rest is working itself out.

1076

Your spiritual path is your inner journey. It will unfold according to your efforts and commitment and cannot be constrained by the fear or judgement of any other.

1077

Believe in your capacity to attract good fortune, lucky breaks and positive twists of fate, knowing that these are expressions of spiritual generosity and goodness in your life.

1078

The oracle indicates material success, financial freedom and positive development in all ways, on all levels.

1079 Have patience, beloved, for the challenge of being an original and independent thinker, is that you sometimes have to wait for the rest of the world to catch up.

Listen to your body and rest when needed, but do not allow your motivation to wane, as great accomplishment is predicted for you. **1080**

1081 The higher workings of karma, mercy and justice are at play and involve more people than yourself, so ask for divine assistance with a matter of concern and trust the Universe has love as its ultimate purpose.

1082 A sacred partnership will empower your soul purpose and shift you into a more prominent position.

Know that you are at the beginning of greater success and will create an impact and have the capacity to further your position in due course. **1083**

1084 Do not compare yourself to others. Trust in the divine timing of your own sacred emergence.

1085

The timing of your path is intertwined with the awakening of the greater collective, but not controlled by the fears or opinions of any other. While you must "wait your turn" to step forward and be seen for who you are, you are free to make as much inner progress as you choose.

1086

A deep and abiding commitment of love and protection shall be offered to you, and you shall feel you have a guardian in the spiritual realms and here on earth.

1087

Calm your worries and turn inward with patience, care and trust, for you already know how to proceed with wisdom.

Success, accomplishment and good
fortune shall be yours.

You shall not be overcome by negativity.

 Nothing from the past shall hold you back.

Your path is guiding you towards fulfilment,
even when you are subject to doubt.

1092 When the way becomes rough or uncertain, prayer opens up the pathway for peace, prosperity and progress.

1093 As you continue to narrow your focus and apply yourself to what you can do in this moment, success is manifesting for you.

1094 The Universe works faithfully for your best interests, and though you may not yet sense it coming, a sign that it's your time is imminent.

1095

Out of the tumultuous and unpredictable workings of life, a positive shift shall emerge, and you will realise that what you felt was a negative sign, was not so at all.

1096 Have compassion for what is going on around you, but do not allow it to overwhelm your heart or distract you from your path.

That which you have sacrificed to make progress on your spiritual path shall be returned to you amplified, in the forms of blessing, protection and peace. **1097**

1098 Approach a practical problem from a spiritual perspective and ask for divine assistance and you'll find it is serving your highest purpose and leading you deeper into peaceful, trustworthy and loving spiritual connection.

1099 Your humanitarian heart and understanding of spiritual laws create a winning combination that shall actively encourage the evolution of the human collective and attract tremendous spiritual aid in support of your higher purpose.

You are going to experience a complete change of consciousness that will recalibrate the frequency of your mind, body and soul to love, peace and happiness. **1100**

1101 When one reaches a new level of spiritual attainment, there is an adjustment period in the outer world, during which one learns to see things in a more positive and helpful light.

1102

Your spiritual guides bring you the message that they can help you whenever you ask for their assistance. Become quiet, reflective and receptive so you can sense their helpful guidance.

1103

Your spiritual guides ask you to give your mental energies a rest so your mind can reset itself into more positive patterns of thought because you have every right to be optimistic.

1104

Your spiritual guides bring you the message that they are assisting you in matters of love, finance and physical wellbeing, helping you to transcend the pain of the past and be open to a new way of being.

1105 Through a lucky break and positive karma, you will find a positive and peaceful path through a stormy or uncertain time.

1106 Follow your heart, and good fortune, success and empowerment shall come to you.

1107 Keeping a goal in your heart, while allowing the path to that goal to be different than you expected, will attract the supportive wisdom of the Universe to your cause.

1108 You do not need to force things to overcome this situation, so let go of trying to control it and connect to the heart wisdom that can show you a more relaxed and responsive way through.

Be willing for life to flow more easily, loosen your grip on the troubles or doubts that your mind has held on to and discover a more grace-filled path. **1109**

 1110 A predestined awakening that will guide your spiritual pathway from darkness to light is taking place now.

1111

Cosmic Wildcard: Anything is possible now, so let go of interpretations about what has been, align yourself with loving frequencies and be ready to enjoy rapid unfoldment in unexpected ways.

ABOUT THE AUTHOR

Alana Fairchild

From the earliest memories I have, I was always in conscious connection with Spirit. It has always been as natural as breathing to me. When something is natural for you, especially if it has been that way since childhood, you can assume for a long time it is natural for everyone. It took me some years to realise my sensitivity, healing ability and natural conscious connection to the spiritual was unusual and could help people. So, I chose to create beautiful offerings to support humans in discovering and manifesting the truth of their hearts. Books, oracle decks, music albums, guided meditations, training programs for healers and more. All are designed to bring out the beauty and truth of your inner divine nature, so you can live with freedom, courage, happiness and peace.

If you would like to find out more, please visit me at my online home:

www.alanafairchild.com

For more information on this
or any Blue Angel Publishing®
release, please visit our
website at:

www.blueangelonline.com